D1329383

WEEP NOT
FOR ME

WEEP NOT FOR ME

Meditations on the Cross and the Resurrection

JOHN V. TAYLOR

XXIII

TWENTY-THIRD PUBLICATIONS

Mystic, Connecticut

North American Edition 1987
Twenty-Third Publications
P.O. Box 180
Mystic, CT 06355
(203) 536-2611

Originally published by World Council
of Churches, © 1986, 150 route de
Ferney, 1211 Geneva 20, Switzerland.

ISBN 0-89622-313-2
Library of Congress Catalog Card Number 86-71639

Table of contents

Introductory Note

Holy Week 1984. The chapel of the Ecumenical Centre in Geneva. A crowd of people, gathered in circular formation, intently listening to a man dressed in a faded purple cassock as he quietly leads them deeper into the mystery of God, of the cross.

For many years, the Worship Committee of the Ecumenical Centre, which houses not only the World Council of Churches but also other ecumenical organizations, had dreamed of having a meditation leader for Holy Week (or rather "Western Holy Week" as we have learned to describe it). We wanted to invite someone to come and share our life and lead us in a time which would deepen our spiritual lives, so often frazzled and dry from bureaucratic and over-busy agendas. We thought of it also as a time to offer something to the wider community of Geneva. The opportunity to realize this came when John V. Taylor, then Bishop of Winchester, announced his retirement early enough for an invitation to be extended to him to come and be our meditation leader in 1984.

So we made our plans and sent out letters and put up posters in all the international organizations and

1

churches and local official places. And people came, and afterwards they came again, bringing their friends, and the community grew as the week went on. A community of seekers, glad and heartened at not being fobbed off with easy answers, seeing in this man, John Taylor, with his scarred eyes and humorous mouth someone who had also suffered and doubted and been tempted, a fellow pilgrim.

For those who are not familiar with John through his long involvement with the ecumenical movement and the churches across the world, it is perhaps helpful to give a brief biographical sketch. Born and brought up in the Church of England, himself the son of a bishop, he went to Uganda as a young married priest and rejoiced in his work as theological educator, drawing on and encouraging the rich African spirituality he found there, especially in the realm of music and drama. "The Passion in Africa" was produced at Mukono theological college and later became a book with superb illustrations. After ten years in Uganda the family returned to England, but later John went back for some research for the International Missionary Council out of which came two of his most famous books, *The Growth of the Church in Buganda* and *The Primal Vision*. Even as recently as 1985, on a British churches visit to South Africa a friend told me that gratitude was being expressed for *The Primal Vision*. It was perhaps here most clearly that one special gift of John's began to be seen — the capacity to listen deeply and with the inner ear of the heart and spirit.

Years of work as Africa secretary, then general secretary of the Church Missionary Society in Britain, meant continual exposure to the world and the church in the world and the constant struggle to see what mission is today. *The Go-between God*, written during these years, is still one of the best books written on the Holy Spirit and Christian mission.

In 1974 John was called to Winchester as Bishop and spent the next ten years there, delighting in opportunities for work with television and in the production of the musical drama of "Passion and Resurrection" to which he alludes in his talks; experiencing too the church at its most basic parish level in the ordinary lives of men and women. Participation in the Melbourne World Mission Conference "Your Kingdom Come" drew him into an ecumenical debate on "power and powerlessness" in correspondence among Kosuke Koyama, Manas Buthelezi and John Yoder, later joined by Allan Boesak. Some strands of the talks he gave in 1984 find early echoes in that discussion.

It was from this wealth of experience and reflection that John shared with us the meditations which follow. We are grateful for permission to publish them, particularly since part of the material will eventually be incorporated in a longer book which will soon be published in Britain.

These talks were given at noon each day in the chapel, following an introductory talk at our normal Monday morning worship service. Thus they form five separate pieces and, as we originally received them, they were interspersed with prayer and silence. We sang, we listened afresh to the gospel narrative of the passion and we brooded on the poems included here. Our themes were around the cross as key — key to the nature of God. This first talk was given, appropriately enough, on All Fools Day, 1 April, when we were pointed to "a reversal of all our assumptions and expectations". The other talks focused on:

— the cross as the key to the mystery of iniquity;
— the cross as the key to our hope of salvation;
— the cross as the way of life through death
   The final meditation was on Holy Thursday and we
ended by a simple act of washing one another's feet.
With towel and water and basin one knelt before
another and *did* that act symbolic of servanthood, the
true mark of the disciples of Christ.

Gwen Cashmore
Geneva, November 1985

1. "Weep not for me"

A large number of people followed him, including women who mourned and wailed for him. Jesus turned and said to them, "Daughters of Jerusalem, do not weep for me; weep for yourselves and for your children. For the time will come when you will say, 'Blessed are the barren women, the wombs that never bore and the breasts that never nursed!' Then they will say to the mountains, 'Fall on us!' and to the hills 'Cover us!' For if men do these things when the tree is green, what will happen when it is dry?"
(Luke 23:27-31)

Do not weep for me. No. Weep for yourselves and for
your children.

This week a large part of the worldwide Christian
fellowship is paying attention in one way or another to
the last days and the last hours of the earthly life of
Jesus of Nazareth. Millions of minds will be focused
for a short while upon his Cross and Passion, perhaps
through hearing again the music of Bach or singing
the hymns of Calvary, or through a fresh recollection of
the images of his death and resurrection as the artists of
many nations have portrayed them. And once again
we may be moved to compassion and horror and
wonder as our thoughts dwell upon his sufferings.
Perhaps we need to hear again his own warning
admonition: Weep not for me.

It is the only divine prohibition in the Passion story.
The crucifixion narrative opens with this word to the
women by the wayside. The story of his resurrection
begins with a similar word to a woman in the garden:
Touch me not. At these tremendous moments, Jesus
says no to the easy spontaneous emotion, the quick
release of tension, because it is misdirected and
because it is dangerous. Tears for the physical
suffering of the Crucified, embraces for the physical
body of the Risen Lord — these are too shallow: they
focus attention on the wrong things.

We should be thankful for this prohibition. We
belong to a culture, especially in the Western lands, in
which feelings have been prostituted. Tears are wrung
from us for our entertainment. We enjoy a good cry —
and feel better afterwards and quickly forget what it was
that moved us. We are accustomed to watching the
misery of others on our TV or cinema screens without
ever having to do anything about it. But it is very rarely

that we weep for truth. It is very rarely that we weep for our sins or for the love of God. Pity is too cheap. We need the bracing realism of Jesus who turned out the professional mourners — Why this crying and commotion?

The demand that Jesus makes from the cross is so stark, so matter of fact, so persistent that it cannot be satisfied by a brief response of our surface emotion. He is looking for nothing less than a change of direction in the quiet depths of our wills.

As we read the story again, incident by incident, we must be struck by the hard fact that two thousand years have not made much difference to humanity. The changes are only on the surface. When armed men get a victim into their hands, handcuffed and alone, they can't resist the urge to knock him about — he's fair game in the back rooms of Caiaphas's house or any other police barracks. Weep for yourselves. When someone who has learned to play the power game finds that his delicately balanced structure of interest is threatened, it is still expedient to wipe out one unimportant but awkward individual to preserve that balance and keep the peace, whether the manipulator is the High Priest of Judaea or the President of where you will. Weep for yourselves. Those who have the power to insist that justice is done, still prefer to wash their hands of the matter, and crowds of ordinary, decent, frightened women and men yell the slogans of the moment rather than stopping to think and stand out against the rest. Weep for yourselves.

The Cross of Jesus Christ cannot be observed objectively from a position of detachment. To be there at all is to be involved, implicated one way or another. That is why all but one of the disciples were not there:

they were not ready to be involved. The daughters of Jerusalem were not ready to be involved, they preferred to pity. Pity is one of the most deceptive of human emotions. It is a half-way stopping place on the way to discipleship. Yet at no time did Jesus ask us to pity him, or to pity his brothers or sisters in whom we are meant to find him.

We are called to feed them and clothe them, visit them in sickness and in prison. We are called to become involved in them at the level of our wills and our action. So if we are to pay attention to his passion and resurrection this week we shall become involved somehow or other. Our whole existence may become involved, since there is no part of it which is untouched by this event.

But we shall not really become involved in the Passion of Jesus unless we also are willing to be involved more deeply in our world. And when I say "more deeply", I mean we must learn to see the sufferings of the hungry and oppressed and powerless in the light of this crucifixion. For that is the true mystery of the Cross. Here every human suffering and every human evil is focused into one single event — the dying of the Son of God. As the light and warmth of the sun spread across the landscape is concentrated through a lens to produce one point of intense heat, so in the Cross of Jesus we see all the wrong and injustice of the long human story, all the agonies and griefs of the human race, focused in upon this one sufferer: the Lamb of God who carries the sin of the world. Here is the meaning of it all. Here is the truth of it all. Here is the way through it all and the promise of ultimate salvation.

We must not be content to form a little cluster of devout people engaged in a religious exercise for the improvement of our souls. If that is all we are doing we shall have no more part in the real event than those wailing daughters of Jerusalem had then. But if we will dare to be honest and to take the whole world into our gaze this week we shall have cause for weeping. "Weep for yourselves and for your children for the days are coming..." so Jesus prophesied the self-destruction of his beloved nation and we who contemplate his Cross again this week are not far from our own self-destruction.

The true perspective of our lives is not the small, moderate bourgeois world that we pretend is ours but a cosmic stage on which the great extremes of the Gospel are stark realities — light and darkness, life and death, luxury and starvation, heaven and perdition. In this struggle of immense opposites the Cross of Jesus Christ towers to its true height. For in the world as it is today nothing can avail to save us but an act of God making available once more to humanity the divine wisdom and strength and love.

Prayer

O Lord God,
whose glory has shone upon us
in the face of Jesus Christ,
and whose nature is made known to us
in the mystery of his Cross;
number us, we pray,
among his faithful followers
for whom nothing matters
but the doing of your will,
in your way,
for your world,
through the same Jesus Christ our Lord.

2. The Cross — Key to the Nature of God

For the message of the Cross is foolishness to those who are perishing, but to us who are being saved it is the power of God. For it is written: "I will destroy the wisdom of the wise; the intelligence of the intelligent I will frustrate."

Where is the wise man? Where is the scholar? Where is the philosopher of this age? Has not God made foolish the wisdom of the world? For since in the wisdom of God the world through its wisdom did not know him, God was pleased through the foolishness of what was preached to save those who believe. Jews demand miraculous signs and Greeks look for wisdom, but we preach Christ crucified: a stumbling-block to Jews and foolishness to Gentiles, but to those whom

11

*God has called, both Jews and Greeks, Christ the
power of God and the wisdom of God. For the
foolishness of God is wiser than man's wisdom, and the
weakness of God is stronger than man's strength.*

*Brothers, think of what you were when you were
called. Not many of you were wise by human
standards; not many were influential; not many were
of noble birth. But God chose the foolish things of
the world to shame the wise; God chose the weak
things of the world to shame the strong. He chose the
lowly things of this world and the despised things —
and the things that are not — to nullify the things that
are, so that no-one may boast before him.*
(1 Cor. 1:18-29)

*To keep me from becoming conceited because of these
surpassingly great revelations, there was given me a
thorn in my flesh, a messenger of Satan, to torment me.
Three times I pleaded with the Lord to take it away
from me. But he said to me, "My grace is sufficient
for you, for my power is made perfect in weakness."
Therefore I will boast all the more gladly about my
weaknesses, so that Christ's power may rest on me.
That is why, for Christ's sake, I delight in weaknesses,
in insults, in hardships, in persecutions, in difficulties.
For when I am weak, then I am strong.*
(2 Cor. 12:7-10)

After the fact of the resurrection had dawned on the
slow minds of the disciples they knew that Jesus and
God were in some profound sense inseparably linked.
"He was taken into heaven" was how they put it.

Jesus and God belonged together forever and always had done so.

What they had seen in the living and dying of Jesus of Nazareth was the true nature of the Heavenly Father he had known so intensely and reflected so faithfully and deliberately.

When they had got over the shock of what they had realized, when they had absorbed it and seen its significance shining round them like fire they put it into a formula as a message for humankind: Jesus is Lord. And the world has misunderstood that message from the very beginning, and the church, yes they themselves the messengers, had difficulty in remembering always the surprise element in the message.

We think we know all about lords. "The Lord" was a common title of the Roman emperor. Lord meant world ruler, ultimate force, absolute control.

We human beings are physically puny in a world of brute force. From our childhood we long for greater power and more perfect control. We admire the strongest, the victor, the one who outsmarts the others. So, with our gift for fantasy, we project those images of domination out into the skies and call it God.

God is imaged as the super-potentate among the emperors, the master-mind over all the clever controllers. God (unlike us) can do exactly as God wants at any moment. God (like our secret wishes) fixes everything. Get him on your side and you can't lose. And what human psychology brought to pass, the philosophers were quick to rationalize.

If Jesus is Lord in that sense then the thirty years of Incarnation were like an exceptional assignment he had to undertake involving a disguise and some temporary hardship and humiliation. His radical reassessment of authority — "In the world kings lord it over their subjects, and those in authority are called their country's benefactors: not so with you. On the contrary the highest among you must bear himself like the youngest, the chief of you like a servant. Here am I among you like a servant" — all this presumably was meant for the duration only. And the victim on the cross was enduring merely the last bad patch before the climax when he could throw off his disguise, mission accomplished, and get back on the throne of the universe. The helplessness and pain tell us nothing new about God.

That is how the church has too often presented the story. But that is not the only way of saying "Jesus is Lord." It can be announced as a reversal of all our assumptions and expectations. *Jesus* is Lord. His unconditional acceptance of all and sundry is the ultimate power. His patient suffering, non-assertive love will have the last word. His inexhaustible endurance will outlast every defeat. That is what the ruler of the universe is like.

John Austin Baker, now Bishop of Salisbury, wrote in *The Foolishness of God*: "The crucified Jesus is the only accurate picture of God the world has ever seen." He echoes the view of C.E. Rolt who in 1913 wrote: "The only omnipotence known to God is the Almighty Power of suffering love."

Theologians and poets have delighted to play with the paradox of the Incarnation: "Our God contracted to a span." But their endless conceits have served to muffle the outrageously unbalanced and unbalancing corrective which the Incarnation makes known. This is more than paradox. In the tug-of-war contrast between human and

divine the tension has slackened because the concept of
God has been shifted. If God was in Christ we have to
come to terms with a God to whom it is natural to be
humble, frustrated and at risk. The coming of Jesus was
a prodigious revelation that turned the previous ideas of
God and of authority on their head.

Professor John McQuarrie has said: "Where we go
wrong is that we bring along some ready-made idea of
God, wherever we may have learned it, and then try to
make Jesus Christ fit in with that idea of God. But if
we take the idea of a *revelation* of God in Christ
seriously, then we must be willing to have our
understanding of God corrected and even revolutionized
by what we learn in Jesus Christ."

What we learn about God in Jesus Christ must
include both the inexhaustible activity of Galilee,
redemptive and life-giving, and the silent passivity of
the passion, hands tied and at the disposal of others.

It may be objected that the revelation of God in
Christ is not to be sought only in what he did and
suffered but also in what he taught.

Surely the God Jesus believed in was the God of the
Old Testament. He appears to have accepted the
teaching of his home and synagogue and did not talk
like someone introducing a new image of God.

If you pause to think about it, a Jew in his
circumstances, whose understanding of God was indeed
different, would not have discarded the scriptures and
the tradition, but rather would build on those elements
in them which tended most closely to the new insight.
And one of the central themes of the Old Testament,
God's covenant with the chosen people, does involve a
tying of his hands with love. The covenant was a
contract and a commitment initiated by God. He was

not bound to set his love upon that particular family and people; he chose to do so. But having gratuitously made them his own he had involved himself forever in their destiny and their sufferings. He had exposed himself to the risk of rejection with no redress, like the faithful husband of a faithless wife.

The note of helpless waiting is heard in several familiar passages. "How can I give you up, O Ephraim? How can I hand you over, O Israel? My heart recoils within me at the thought, for I am God and not man, the Holy One in your midst, and I will not come to destroy." "Now you who live in Jerusalem and you men of Judah, judge between me and my vineyard. What more could have been done for my vineyard that I did not do to it? Why, when I look for it to bear grapes, did it yield wild grapes?"

Though Jesus is not reported as having dwelt on the theme of covenant, apart from one momentous exception, his spiritual affinity was clearly with that school of prophecy in the Old Testament — the book of Deuteronomy, Jeremiah and Ezekiel — for which the covenent was a central theme.

Very well, then; let us look at his teaching in more detail. The things he appears to have *avoided* saying are an indication of the image of God which he felt to be most true. His theme was the kingdom, yet a king and his court appear in very few of the parables that deal with that theme. Rabbis of his time used a parable about a king hiring labourers for his vineyard, but when Jesus told a similar story the central figure is a landowner. "King" and "Father" were both epithets used frequently in Jewish prayers of the time, but he chose only the second. Furthermore, the fathers in his parables, though they certainly have authority, are all subject to the whims and refusals of their children. The best-known is depicted as waiting, ever watchful for his son's return, and then pleading with the elder brother. Another father has his request refused at first by one son, forgotten or neglected by the other. One father responds to his children's demands for bread or fish while another is roused from the family bed by an importunate and improvident neighbour.

The image of an authority figure exposed to risk is repeated in the farmer who, growing corn, and finding it intersown with tares, decides to leave them alone till harvest. This is the hazard in the unconditional inclusiveness which Jesus extended to people without test or question. Other parables made the same point: indiscriminate acceptance will land you with a traitor eventually.

A God who cannot set a limit to his self-giving, who cannot ensure himself against suffering, who cannot be wholly in control of the relationships he initiates — what strange God is this? (2 Cor. 12:7-10)

Some months ago I was asked by a friend to visit a young couple whose two-year old daughter had been found dead in her cot. They were still stunned and haunted by the old question Why?, and sometimes, Why her? I simply could not offer them the conventional reassurance about it all being in God's providence, a mystery now but one day to be seen as part of a loving plan. I know that many good souls derive lasting comfort from such counsel, and it certainly squares with a good deal in the Bible, and is to be found in many books of devotion and pastoral practice. But to me it has become unconvincing and strained and suggests a picture of God I find impossible to love, arrogant though that sounds. I said to them instead that their child's death was a tragic accident, an unforeseeable failure in the functioning of the little body; that, so far from being willed or planned by God It was for him a disaster and a frustration of his will for life and fulfilment, just as it was for them, that God shared their pain and loss and was with them in it. I went on to say that God is not a potentate ordering this or that to happen, but that the world is full of chance and accident and God has let it be so because that is the only sort of world in which freedom, development, responsibility and love could come into being, but that God was committed to this kind of world in love and to each person in it, and was with them in this tragedy, giving himself to them in fortitude and healing and faith to help them through. And their child was held in that same caring, suffering love.

Such an approach to the problem lays a greater responsibility on us as human beings, and this is in keeping with the gospel. We see the element of human responsibility and cooperation with God most clearly in Jesus himself. He did not expect life to work out to his advantage. He worked not a single miracle for himself. "Do you suppose that I cannot appeal to my Father who would at once send to my aid more than twelve legions of angels?" But how then could the scriptures be fulfilled — not only the scriptures about the death and the sacrifice, but the whole witness of the scriptures to the purpose of the creation and the way the world actually is. Towers do not fall on specially selected victims. They fall by accident or from sinful carelessness. So Jesus takes responsibility for events himself in such practical ways as having a donkey standing ready for his ride into the capital and a prearranged guide to the room he had booked for the Last Supper. And on the cross we see the ultimate reversal of the old idea of providence. The anguished, all too natural prayer was offered, "If it be possible...", and it was not possible. There was no intervention, only the terrible silence and a gazing into darkness. And on either side of that silence there was pain — the human suffering and the divine as God and Jesus held firm to the intention that had been there before the foundation of the world: Love bent on creating the possibility of an answering love. So we do not see God averting evil to protect his human child; we see him absorbing evil, letting it come upon him in the person of his human child, and so turning the evil into overwhelming good. That is the essence of forgiveness, the forgiveness of men and women by God and, dare I say it, the forgiveness of God by men and women — God reconciling the world to himself.

A Hymn to the Creator

Morning glory, starlit sky,
Leaves in springtime, swallows' flight,
Autumn gales, tremendous seas,
Sounds and scents of summer night;

Soaring music, tow'ring words,
Art's perfection, scholar's truth,
Joy supreme of human love,
Memory's treasure, grace of youth;

Open, Lord, are these, Thy gifts,
Gifts of love to mind and sense;
Hidden is love's agony,
Love's endeavour, love's expense.

Love that gives gives ever more,
Gives with zeal, with eager hands,
Spares not, keeps not, all outpours,
Ventures all, its all expends.

Drained is love in making full;
Bound in setting others free;
Poor in making many rich;
Weak in giving power to be.

Therefore He Who Thee reveals
Hangs, O Father, on that Tree
Helpless; and the nails and thorns
Tell of what Thy love must be.

Thou art God; no monarch Thou
Thron'd in easy state to reign;
Thou art God, Whose arms of love
Aching, spent, the world sustain.

> From W.H. Vanstone
> *Love's Endeavour, Love's Expense*[1]

A Litany

Eternal, Holy God, you revealed the hidden mystery
of your being in the face of Jesus Christ,
and showed your true glory in his cross.

---

[1] *The Response of Being to the Love of God*, Darton, Longman and
Todd, London, 1977.

Lord, we believe —
Help our unbelief

Inexhaustible Creator and Source of Life,
you dignify your universe with the awful gift
of freedom and you wait in mercy
till it freely returns your love.
  Lord, we believe —
  Help our unbelief

You bound yourself in a Covenant
with your disobedient people; your hands were tied
by your faithfulness and you could not give them up.
  Lord, we believe —
  Help our unbelief

In all our afflictions you are afflicted,
and not one person suffers but you feel the pain.
  Lord, we believe —
  Help our unbelief

Eternal Word, you entered the weakness of our human
condition, you humbled yourself
even to death on a cross,
because this is eternally your nature.
  Lord, we believe —
  Help our unbelief

The poor are your people because they share
your powerlessness; the oppressed find you near
because they know your rejectedness.
  Lord, we believe —
  Help our unbelief

Your foolishness, Father, is wiser than humanity;
your weakness, Lord, is stronger than humanity.
Lord, we believe —
Help our unbelief

You invite us in Christ to stay awake with you
in your endurance, but we turn away
to our idols of power and violence.
Lord, we believe —
Help our unbelief

You call us in Christ to wait with you
in your patient hope,
but we choose to worship efficiency and speed.
Lord, we believe —
Help our unbelief

Teach us to stand with you in Christ;
fill us with the divine love that bears and believes
and hopes and endures all things
yet never comes to an end.
Lord, we believe —
Help our unbelief

Christians and Pagans

We go to God when we are sore bestead,
Pray to him for succour, for his peace, for bread,
For mercy for the sick, sinning, or dead;
We all do so, Christians and unbelieving.

We go to God when we are sore bestead,
Find him poor and scorned, without shelter or bread,
Whelmed under weight of the wicked, the weak, the
   dead;
Christians stand by God in his hour of grieving.

God goes to every one when they are sore bestead,
Feedeth body and spirit with his bread;
For Christians, pagans alike he hangeth dead,
And both alike forgiving.

Dietrich Bonhoeffer
Widerstand und Ergebung

3. The Cross — Key to the Mystery of Iniquity

As for you, you were dead in your transgressions and sins, in which you used to live when you followed the ways of this world and of the ruler of the kingdom of the air, the spirit who is now at work in those who are disobedient. All of us also lived among them at one time, gratifying the cravings of our sinful nature and following its desires and thoughts. Like the rest, we were by nature objects of wrath. But because of his great love for us, God, who is rich in mercy, made us alive with Christ even when we were dead in transgressions — it is by grace you have been saved. And God raised us up with Christ and seated us with him in the heavenly realms in Christ Jesus, in order that in the coming ages he might show the

incomparable riches of his grace, expressed in his
kindness to us in Christ Jesus. (Eph. 2:1-7)

There is a quite extraordinary amount of hostility and
hate in the Passion story. I realized this with surprise
when I produced the drama of Jesus' death and
resurrection three years ago in a modern church
opera. Abuse and cruelty are piled upon the helpless,
silent prisoner by one group after another, and it is all
undeserved and pointless. Why did so much hatred boil
over upon this man of all men? Why should one of his
closest companions, the man he trusted with the
common purse, deliberately agree with Jesus' enemies
to help them to carry out this capture? Was it envy
or fear? Why should the teachers of the moral law,
the Pharisees with their passion for spiritual revival,
be so set upon destroying this young rabbi? Even if he
was a bit unorthodox, need they have over-reacted so
extremely?

And have we ever explained satisfactorily the
implacable determination of that high-priestly family
to drive Pilate to impose the death penalty? Wasn't the
terrible flogging enough? Luigi Santucchi, the Italian
novelist, says: "We can minister to God and serve him
in our own way but we have a horror of meeting him.
If he comes too near we have only one way of
defending ourselves from him, Caiaphas's way — by
killing him, killing him even in the name of God,
shouting at him that it's blasphemy to appear alive in
our midst."

Why should the attendant guards in Caiaphas's hall
suddenly start to beat their prisoner about the head?
Why should Roman soldiers who had nothing but their
stolid duty to carry out that morning — a routine

business for them — why should they turn against their half-fainting victim with another vicious burst of bullying?

We haven't really answered this question after all these centuries; for the cold facts of the reports of Amnesty International remind us that, even while we are sitting here some man or woman in some police post or military guardroom anywhere in the world is being battered or tortured by people for no particular reason except that he or she is at their mercy. Or rather, there is very often one particular reason — and that is the enduring, unbroken, non-aggressive humanity of the victim. If you read those terrible reports — or if you are honest enough to read your own heart — you will notice that if the prisoner's control breaks down in cringing submission or screaming rage, the aggressor's cruelty often evaporates, for there's nothing left to destroy. But when the victim neither grovels nor retaliates nor hates, but goes on offering a relationship, insists on a relationship, then the attacker grows more vicious and mindless because he is motivated by a great fear. He grows more vicious because he knows now that he is inwardly weaker than his victim. He dare not accept the person-to-person relationship that this bleeding humanity is holding out to him. It is generally admitted that that is why Steve Biko had to die. It is certain that that is why such hatred was turned upon Jesus. We have a horror of meeting God. If he comes too near we have only one way of defending ourselves, Caiaphas's way. The weakness of God mediated through a human sufferer is stronger than any human power.

But this still does not wholly explain what made the rabble of ordinary citizens clamour so greedily for Jesus' execution. What did they have against him?

We need not press too far the contrast between the

Hosannas of five days earlier and the blood lust of this
Friday morning. Mob feelings are unthinking and
bewildered, and the crowds in Pilate's courtyard may not
have included many of those Galilean pilgrims who
cheered his entry into the city. These were the shopkeep-
ers and artisans and housewives of Jerusalem, the unem-
ployed and the disaffected perhaps, nervous, suspicious,
like dry tinder ready to be fired by any political spark.
They probably knew nothing about Jesus. They had no
idea what they were doing when they yelled "Crucify
him!" But they tipped the balance and the Roman gover-
nor decided that he must condemn Jesus to death. They
were implicated in this appalling injustice, they rein-
forced the very system that was oppressing them, without
any understanding of the part they were playing.

This tells us so much about the nature of evil. It
explains why the worst wrongs are often done from the
best motives. It explains why the institutions we establish
to serve our ideals of justice, the pursuit of truth,
development, security, or the worship of God, become
the destroyers of those very ideals. This fact was
brilliantly brought to light by a Muslim novelist in Egypt
in the 1960s, Kamel Hussein, in the novel he wrote
about Good Friday called *City of Wrong*:

> The day was a Friday. But it was quite unlike any
> other day. It was a day when men went very
> grievously astray, so far astray in fact that they
> involved themselves in the utmost iniquity. Evil
> overwhelmed them and they were blind to the truth,
> though it was as clear as the morning sky. Yet for all
> that they were people of religion and character and the
> most careful of men about following the right. They
> were endeared to the good and none were given to
> profounder meditation. They were of all people most
> meticulous, tenderly affected towards their nation and

their fatherland, sincere in their religious practice and characterized by fervour, courage and integrity. Yet this thorough competence in their religion did not save them from wrong-doing, nor immunize their minds from error. Their sincerity did not guide them to the good. They were a people who took counsel among themselves, yet their counsels led them astray. Their Roman overlords, too, were masters of law and order, yet these proved their undoing. The people of Jerusalem were caught that day in a vortex of seducing factors and, taken unawares amid them, they faltered. Lacking sound and valid criteria of action, they foundered utterly, as if they had been a people with neither reason nor religion.

They considered that reason and religion laid upon them obligation that transcended the dictates of conscience. They did not realize that when men suffer the loss of conscience there is nothing that can replace it. For human conscience is a torch of the light of God and without it there is no guidance for mankind. When humanity has no conscience to guide it, every virtue collapses, every good turns to evil and all intelligence is crazed.

On that day men willed to murder their conscience and that decision constitutes the supreme tragedy of humanity. The events of that day do not simply belong to the annals of the early centuries. They are disasters renewed daily in the life of every individual. Men to the end of time will be contemporaries of that memorable day, perpetually in danger of the same sin and wrong-doing into which the inhabitants of Jerusalem then fell. The same darkness will be theirs until they are resolute not to transgress the bounds of conscience.

Another remarkable novel on the same theme appeared in Japan at about the same time. It was called *The Sea and Poison* and the author was Shusaku Endo, better known for his great novel *Silence*. *The Sea and Poison* tells the story of a small hospital during the war where the medical superintendent was ordered to carry out surgical experiments on American prisoners involving their eventual death. For every member of the hospital staff it was an obscene denial of their professional scruples, yet because no one openly admitted what was going on, and because what each one had to do was only a slight deviation from the normal correct routine, everyone acquiesced without exception. There was a universal complicity.

Now that is the verdict passed by the death of Jesus Christ. That is the diagnosis of our human condition pronounced by that event. The Cross is the key to the mystery of iniquity.

But do you see what this means? A simplistic view of evil in any situation that confronts us is no longer an option for the Christian. As we say in English, there are no "goodies" and "baddies". There are no absolute villains and no absolute heroes. None is absolutely innocent or absolutely guilty. The watchword of Christian faith — "no distinction, no discrimination", which is rooted in the way Jesus himself treated people, and which we welcome when it is applied to race and colour, or to men and women — that central watchword has to be applied also to our judgment of the good and the bad in every situation of conflict. "There is no distinction", says Paul to the Romans, "for all alike have sinned." This does not absolve us from the conflict. We still know who are the people and what are the structures against which we have to contend. But we shall actually fight more effectively through recognizing in ourselves as well as in those others the things we are fighting against. We shall be armed with new weapons through understanding in our own experience how the evil attitudes and the commitment to injustice took root. We shall discern more accurately the target for our attack when we see that we are not fighting flesh and blood, but ancient evil in the very fabric of earth and heaven.

And our victories, when we win them, will not be turned into defeat through the corruption inherent in our own power if we have truly accepted the truth of our own complicity and let it bring forth in us, as it is bound to do, the spirit of understanding and forgiveness. For we shall have fought as those who know in themselves that the hardness of the unjust, the cruelty of the oppressor, the angry violence of the powerful is the bitter fruit of their own hidden pain and fear. For every human being is on a cross of some sort — Pilate and Caiaphas and Herod and Judas — and Jesus was the one who understood that as the nails were driven in. We acknowledge this without noticing it every time we recite the ancient creed of Nicea: "He was made man and was crucified."

Our inner pain and fear — our individual private crucifixions — give another answer to the question with which we started: Why is there so much hostility and hate in the Passion story? With whom were they so angry? Or, to bring that question nearer home — who is it that we are so angry with for a lot of the time when we are submerged in a black cloud of hostility and antagonism which we are frightened even to admit, or when the inner rage is held back and turns into deep depression from which we are powerless to break free, who is it we really hate?

Neville Ward in his book on the Rosary, *5 for Sorrow, 10 for Joy*, says: "It is probable that we fear

the world within as much as the world without,
especially the accumulations of dismay and anger
deposited in our lives as life has flowed by uncaught,
unused, carrying so much out of sight. There is so
much for us all to forgive. We can see at any rate that
much of our hostility towards life and people is really
our disapproval of the way things are. Ultimately it is
God who is responsible for this and much of our
hostility is really meant for him."

Does that shock you? Do you want to deny it?
Perhaps you never swear, not even when you are by
yourself. But if you do, or if you've overheard other
people's explosions of rage and frustration, you'll
remember that the words we use are either the very
blunt sex words which are an outburst against the
restraints of polite society, or the divine name — God!
Christ! — and sometimes a combination of both. It is a
bit frightening to realize that we are actually yelling at
God. So we look the other way and call it swearing.
But what is swearing? It means taking an oath, and an
oath is a word that God is meant to hear.

In Holy Week of all times let's admit the truth that
deep inside ourselves we have carried, sometimes at
least, an enormous resentment and anger against God —
or if it's easier to say it, against life. That is what
boiled around Jesus Christ as they lifted him up on the
Cross. "It's God they ought to crucify instead of you
and me." It was God we crucified that day.

And how does God meet our enmity? He takes it into
himself. Jesus speaks not *to* the raging irrational hearts
that are crying against him but he speaks about them.
He doesn't answer back, he answers for them: "Father,
forgive them because they don't know..."

Was he making excuses? Yes. That is what love
does. But love is not blind, it was not merely an

excuse. He was putting their rage and cruelty and hardness and hatred into a new light, the light of a more complete truth, of a perfect understanding and acceptance.

A Litany

We confess to you, Lord, what we are:
We are not the people we like others to think we are;
We are afraid to admit even to ourselves what lies
in the depths of our souls.
Give us a clean heart, O God,
And renew a right spirit within us.

But we do not want to hide our true selves from you.
We believe that you know us as we are,
and yet you love us.
Give us a clean heart, O God,
And renew a right spirit within us.

Help us not to shrink from self-knowledge:
teach us to respect ourselves for your sake.
Give us a clean heart, O God,
And renew a right spirit within us.

Give us the courage to put our trust
in your guiding power.
Raise us out of the paralysis of guilt
into the freedom and energy of forgiven people.
Give us a clean heart, O God,
And renew a right spirit within us.

And for those who through long habit
find forgiveness hard to accept,
we ask you to break their bondage and set them free.

Give us a clean heart, O God,
And renew a right spirit within us.

Lord God almighty, forgive your church
its wealth among the poor,
its fear among the unjust,
its cowardice among the oppressed.
Give us a clean heart, O God,
And renew a right spirit within us.

Forgive us, your children,
our lack of confidence in you,
our lack of hope in your reign,
our lack of faith in your presence,
our lack of trust in your mercy.
Give us a clean heart, O God,
And renew a right spirit within us.

Restore us to your covenant with your people;
bring us to true repentance;
teach us to accept the sacrifice of Christ;
make us strong with the comfort of your Holy Spirit.
Give us a clean heart, O God,
And renew a right spirit within us.

Break us where we are proud,
Make us where we are weak,
Shame us where we trust ourselves,
Blame us where we have lost ourselves;
Through Jesus Christ our Lord. [1]

---

[1] The first part of this litany is reproduced from *Risk*, Geneva, WCC, Vol. 11, Nos 2-3, 1975, p. 69. The second part is from *Contemporary Prayers for Public Worship*, ed. Caryl Micklem, London, SCM Press, 1967: for the USA Wm B. Eerdmans, Grand Rapids, Michigan.

4. The Cross — Key to Our Hope and Salvation

In the year that King Uzziah died, I saw the Lord seated on a throne, high and exalted, and the train of his robe filled the temple. Above him were seraphs, each with six wings: with two wings they covered their faces, with two they covered their feet, and with two they were flying. And they were calling to one another: "Holy, holy, holy is the Lord Almighty; the whole earth is full of his glory."

At the sound of their voices the doorposts and thresholds shook and the temple was filled with smoke. "Woe to me!" I cried. "I am ruined! For I am a man of unclean lips, and I live among a people of unclean lips, and my eyes have seen the

King, the Lord Almighty." Then one of the seraphs
flew to me with a live coal in his hand, which he
had taken with tongs from the altar. With it he
touched my mouth and said, "See, this has touched
your lips; your guilt is taken away and your sin
atoned for."

Then I heard the voice of the Lord saying,
"Whom shall I send? And who will go for us?"
And I said, "Here am I. Send me!" He said, "Go
and tell this people: 'Be ever hearing, but never
understanding; be ever seeing, but never perceiving.'
Make the heart of this people calloused; make their
ears dull and close their eyes. Otherwise they might
see with their eyes, hear with their ears, understand
with their hearts, and turn and be healed."

Then I said, "For how long, O Lord?" And he
answered: "Until the cities lie ruined and without
inhabitant, until the houses are left deserted and the
fields ruined and ravaged, until the Lord has sent
everyone far away and the land is utterly forsaken.
And though a tenth remains in the land, it will
again be laid waste." (Isa. 6:1-13)

As they led him away, they seized Simon from Cyrene,
who was on his way in from the country, and put the
cross on him and made him carry it behind Jesus. A
large number of people followed him, including women
who mourned and wailed for him. Jesus turned and said
to them, "Daughters of Jerusalem, do not weep for me;
weep for yourselves and for your children. For the time
will come when you will say, 'Blessed are the barren
women, the wombs that never bore and the breasts that
never nursed!' Then they will say to the mountains,
'Fall on us!' and to the hills 'Cover us!'

For if men do these things when the tree is green,
what will happen when it is dry?"

*Two other men, both criminals, were also led out
with him to be executed. When they came to the place
called the Skull, there they crucified him, along with the
criminals — one on his right, the other on his left.
Jesus said, "Father, forgive them, for they do not know
what they are doing." And they divided up his clothes
by casting lots.* (Luke 23:26-34)

In these meditations I don't want to make the meaning
of Christ's death more complicated than it actually is,
for if we lose the harsh simplicity of the story it has
no power to change our attitudes and drive us to
commitment in action. So let us get back to the simple
fact that those who were in various positions of power
got rid of Jesus because they were threatened by what
he stood for. His death is a supreme example of
injustice. It stands for all injustice.

It was a judicial murder like tens of thousands of
others, and one can quite legitimately say that the only
reason it has anything to do with us today is that what
he stood for is still so convincing and so necessary for
the future of humanity that we are compelled to take
our stand with him even though it invites the same
opposition. In that case the astounding truth of his
resurrection both sets the seal of God's endorsement on
what Jesus stood for and assures us of his living
companionship to support us in the same struggle.

We must honestly admit that there are problems
concerning the message of Jesus of Nazareth, and it
may not be possible to say with complete certainty how
he understood his task and how he set about it. So there
is room for some hesitation in what we assert. But we
can say confidently that Jesus proclaimed the arrival of
the new age of the reign of God; that he himself
possessed an intense intuitive awareness of the reality

and presence of God, and that he constantly offended
the guardians of morality by his unconditional
acceptance of, and association with, the questionable
and marginalized members of society. If one brings
those three clear facts together to make a coherent
message and way of life, it goes something like this:
The kingdom of God, the looked-for messianic age,
which entailed an end of the world and a new
beginning, was about to dawn. It was at hand. That
particular time factor is important for the whole gospel
of salvation, and we need to grasp it. It is both here and
not quite here. The light of a new day is spreading
across the sky, though its sun has not yet risen. Yet that
sunrise is now so near and so certain that it's time
already to start living the life of the new day, the life of
the new age. And, since it is God's new age, the time
of God's reign, to live in it in anticipation of its arrival
means quite simply to treat everyone here and now as
God treats people. For citizens of this kingdom model
themselves on the king. It is no longer problematic to
do so. No longer do people need the precepts of the law
and its professional teachers to tell them what God is
like, for he is now so near, so directly knowable as
Jesus knew him in his own experience, that anyone can
see what he is like and then go and do likewise. The
nearness of the kingdom was the nearness of God and
the life of the kingdom was the *imitatio Dei*. "Be
merciful as your heavenly Father is merciful." "Let
there be no limit to your goodness as there is no limit to
your Father's goodness." "Love your enemies and pray
for your persecutors; only so can you be children of
your heavenly Father who makes his sun shine on good
and bad alike and sends the rain on the honest and the
dishonest."

And as Jesus taught, so he lived. His acceptance of the unacceptable was a deliberate doing of what he saw the Father doing. His meals shared with sinners and outcastes were a reflection of his own perception of God as a father who prepares a feast to welcome his erring son. The whole motley crowd that sat around him as he taught were his brothers and sisters and his mother, because they were his Father's children. Does this sound sentimental or inadequate as a motivation for today's struggles for justice? Call it, perhaps, Franciscan, and you come nearer the truth. It bases everything on a great simplicity that even a child can grasp, but it is tough as nails, tough as wood and nails. It strips our concern for justice of all sophisticated argument and ideology that might wear thin under disappointment or pain. It identifies the passion for justice with the love of God; it identifies good news for the poor and the liberation of the captives with the celebration of the Lord's jubilee year; it commits Christians to the one unarguable and irreducible manifesto — "on earth as in heaven."

If there had been any idealistic sentimentality in the message Jesus preached in Galilee it would have culminated gloriously in that moment of transfiguration on the mountain top. There the disciples could have been satisfied with a splendid apotheosis of the messenger of love and simplicity. And down in the valley a lunatic boy and a whole lunatic world would have remained unsaved. The sentimentalist Peter would gladly have remained there — and he spoke for a large part of the church in all ages. But the mind of Jesus was set upon a different hill, and he took them down to start the journey towards it.

Jesus died for justice rooted in love. He died for

justice rooted in the nature of God. He died for the incomparable value of the individual person, derived from the human capacity for relationship with other persons and with God which is what we mean by the "image of God". He died to save that image, that capacity for relationship, from defacement, either by the self-induced distortion of sin or the dehumanization of being sinned against. He died to restore the freedom and responsibility which is the necessary condition for love.

There are many people committed to the struggle for freedom and justice without this reference to God. We must both welcome and admire their devotion. But without any superior condescension towards them, we must hold fast to the reference to God not merely as a pious option but as the essential mainspring of our struggle. For Jesus it was all rooted in his knowledge of the nature of God, and it must be so for us. So far from being a distraction or a softening of our effort, the Christian perspective is a unique source of realism. It saves us from a sentimental idealization of justice.

I spoke earlier about the particular time factor in Jesus' understanding of the gospel of the kingdom. It is both here and not quite here. It is near enough and certain enough to justify our courage in starting now to live the life of the kingdom. But the hour of fulfilment is still not yet. We live in the half-light of eschatological time, the "almost but not quite" of the hour before sunrise, in which the repeated command of Jesus is: Keep awake — watch — wait — endure. This sunrise theme is brought out clearly in that great passage in the Epistle to the Romans which brought Saint Augustine to conversion: "Remember how critical the moment is. It is time for you to wake out of sleep for deliverance, salvation, is nearer to us now than it was when first we believed. It is far on in the night. Day is near. Near but not yet. But near enough for us to throw off the deeds of darkness and put on our armour as soldiers of the light." Armour, not wedding garments. Because we live in the not yet.

This passage is a repetition of what Paul had just written before his intervention on the position of the Jewish dispensation. "We have been saved, though only in hope. Now to see is no longer to hope: why should a man endure and wait for what he already sees? But if we hope for something we do not yet see, then, in waiting for it we show our endurance."

I hesitate to dwell on this truth because the church is not yet nerved with conviction enough for the struggle for justice rooted in love, and may so readily grasp any theology that seems to excuse a continuing lack of conviction. But truth is not negotiable, and we can surely trust the truth of Christ. The cross of Jesus commits us unquestionably to the struggle for justice and identification with the victims of oppression, deprivation and discrimination. And there will be victories, as there have been already in history. But the end is not yet. A world in which human beings treat one another as God treats people is not just round the corner. It is not that sort of struggle. It is a struggle that must be maintained to the end of time. For time itself lies in the dimension of "near but not yet". Even the resurrection took place in the hour before the sun had risen, while it was yet dark. Because the resurrection of Jesus is a promise and a guarantee, but it is not the end of the story. The English poet of the 1940s and 50s, David Gascoyne, wrote with a fine sense of paradox:

That there is Justice in the world
Even the fool who hath said in his heart

There is no God
Would be unlikely wholly to deny:
But if he did, even he would not be such a fool
As the man who declares that there is justice in
    the world
And that he can not only see it plainly
    but must proceed to administer it with perfect
    justice.

There is no perfectly just man
Because the vision of Justice is the pleasure of God
    alone.
And that is why the divine part in all men
Longs to see justice and to live by it;
While the enemy of God that is in each of us
Is always trying to make us satisfied
    with what we can see of Justice without God,
As though He were bound to ratify automatically
Whatever a man-made judge with his own reason
    decides is just
Provided a sufficiently large number of other men
    be persuaded to agree with him. [1]

Justice — the realization of the relationships of
heaven here on earth — is a vision to struggle for and
journey towards. Justice is the corporate face of love.
Does this then mean that the realization of love is also
a vision, also endlessly postponed? The answer to that
question is the Cross.

    Love is the anticipation of justice before its
realization. Love can and does flower in the dark before
the dawn. That is its pain and its glory. Love comes to
its triumph while it is still on the cross.

    Archibald Macleish wrote a strange and beautiful play

---

[1] "Fragments Towards a Religio Poetae", *Collected Poems*, ed.
Robin Skelton, London, Oxford University Press, 1965, pp. 117-18.

around the story of Job, which he called JB. JB is a
prosperous banker, on whom one disaster falls after
another, as happened to Job in the Bible story.
Everything finally hangs on the relationship between JB
and his wife Sarah. She stands by him and supports him
to the limit, but when it seems to her that her husband
is acquiescing in a lie about existence her patience
breaks, and she begs him to face facts and curse an
unjust God and die. Then she runs off. Later, when JB
has sunk deeper in despair but is still unbroken, she
returns carrying a broken twig with a few blossoms on
it. JB questions her.

"Curse God and die, you said to me." "Yes," she
replies. "You wanted justice, didn't you? There isn't
any. There's the world. Cry for justice and the stars
will stare until your eyes sting. Weep, enormous winds
will thrash the water. Cry in sleep for your lost
children, snow will fall. Snow will fall." JB: "Why did
you leave me alone?" Sarah: "I loved you. I couldn't
help you any more. You wanted justice and there was
none — only love."

That is no cheap resolution. The problem remains.
The play only states priorities. The cross of Jesus also
doesn't answer the questions, doesn't open the gates of
justice — it states the priorities, and dictates the
methods we must use.

Listening

I am silent	On top of this hill
but the world is not	the heavens open
I pause to listen and	to enfold me
the burning heat	In a caressing embrace
the midday breeze	of eternal bliss

Striking the strings
of the virgin bush
provoke songs of joy
from living things
big and small
In soothing melody
and vibrant rhythm
Speeding cars
Labouring planes
Testify to proximate
bustling city life
Gnawing sound
of feeding ants
Sweet breath of life
from widespread petals
sailing butterfly
sucking bee
A silent footfall
on the polished lawn
Shatters the silence
of my restless soul
Lord I hear now
I am not alone with you
I am my brother's keeper.
Here I stand

Free at last, Free at last
But no
I must descend
to the metropolitan
confusion
the ecclesiastical division
the multi-racial disharmony
to the one-sided
economic rat race
to the hands
Reaching out
Fervently pleading
to be rescued
from the mouth
of the hungry whale
to the weary feet
and aching shoulders
"HOW much longer Lord?
You carried your cross
for half-an-hour
We've carried ours
for a century",
to the depth of Sheoul
to the pit of fire
My brother is there.

Sitiveni Ratuvili, Fiji

Litany I

O Lord, our hearts are heavy with the sufferings
of the ages, with the crusades and the holocausts

of a thousand thousand years.
The blood of the victims is still warm,
The cries of anguish still fill the night.

    To you we lift our outspread hands.

    We thirst for you in a thirsty land.

O Lord, who loves us as a father, who cares for us
as a mother, who came to share our life as a brother,
we confess before you our failure to live
    as your children,
brothers and sisters bound together in love.

    To you we lift our outspread hands.

    We thirst for you in a thirsty land.

We have squandered the gift of life.
The good life of some is built on the pain of many;
the pleasure of a few on the agony of millions.

    To you we lift our outspread hands.

    We thirst for you in a thirsty land.

We worship death in our quest to possess
ever more things; we worship death
in our hankering after our own security,
our own survival, our own peace,
as if life were divisible, as if love were divisible,
as if Christ had not died for all of us.

    To you we lift our outspread hands.

    We thirst for you in a thirsty land.

O Lord, forgive our life-denying pursuit of life,
and teach us anew what it means to be your children.

To you we lift our outspread hands

We thirst for you in a thirsty land. [2]

Litany II

Lord, we remember the millions in our world
who must go hungry today,
all those who do not have even the basic necessities
of life, and for whom life itself has become a
burden.
Out of the depths we cry to you, Lord,
Hear our cry and listen to our prayer.

Lord, we remember all those who, because of their
  caste
or class, colour or sex, are exploited and
  marginalized —
the forces of oppression that trample on people and
the unjust systems which break the spirit of people,
and rob them of their rights and dignity.
Out of the depths we cry to you, Lord,
Hear our cry and listen to our prayer.

---

[2] From *Jesus Christ — the Life of the World*, a worship book for the
Sixth Assembly of the World Council of Churches, Vancouver
1983, Geneva, WCC, 1983, p.26.

Lord, we bring before you the churches and the
Christian people around the world.
Often we have remained silent, passing by
on the other side; often we have been indifferent;
often we have been part of the forces that destroy
   life.
   Out of the depths we cry to you, Lord,
   Hear our cry and listen to our prayer.

Lord, we call to mind all authority that treats people
   as nobodies —
Military regimes and dictatorships,
lonely prisons and unjust laws;
the war industry and political greed.
   Out of the depths we cry to you, Lord,
   Hear our cry and listen to our prayer.

Lord, we affirm with hope your presence in the world.
You see the wounded and the broken, and say —
"These are my brothers and sisters."
   Lord, inspire us with your love,
   challenge us with your truth,
   empower us with your strength
   to live for life in the midst of death.[3]

---

[3] Intercession for Asia Sunday, 3 June 1984, *CCA News*, April
1984, Vol. 19, No. 4.

5. The Cross — the Way of Life through Death

Now there were some Greeks among those who went up to worship at the Feast. They came to Philip, who was from Bethsaida in Galilee, with a request. "Sir," they said, "we would like to see Jesus." Philip went to tell Andrew; Andrew and Philip in turn told Jesus.

Jesus replied, "The hour has come for the Son of Man to be glorified. I tell you the truth, unless a grain of wheat falls to the ground and dies, it remains only a single seed. But if it dies, it produces many seeds. The man who loves his life will lose it, while the man who hates his life in this world will keep it for eternal life. Whoever serves me must follow me; and where I am, my servant also will be. My Father will honour the one who serves me.

*"Now my heart is troubled, and what shall I say?
'Father, save me from this hour'? No, it was for this
very reason I came to this hour. Father, glorify your
name!"*

*Then a voice came from heaven, "I have glorified
it, and will glorify it again."* (John 12:20-28)

*Or don't you know that all of us who were baptized
into Christ Jesus were baptized into his death? We
were therefore buried with him through baptism into
death in order that, just as Christ was raised from the
dead through the glory of the Father, we too may live a
new life.*

*If we have been united with him like this in his
death, we will certainly also be united with him in
his resurrection.* (Rom. 6:3-5)

"The last enemy to be overcome is death," said St Paul.
It is the last to be overcome, not because we meet it
only at the end of our lives, but because its power
over us is more persistent and pervasive than that of
any other foe. So much human aggression or greed or
selfishness or arrogance arises from our dread of the
annihilation which is death. Let's face it, it is bound to
make us afraid, whatever our philosophy. The thought
of not being any more haunted many of the most
sensitive playwrights and novelists of the existentialist
period. "I'm going to die", says Pizarro in *The Royal
Hunt of the Sun*, "and thought of that dark has for years
rotted everything for me, all simple joy in life." The
point of that admission lies in the fact that Pizarro was
the conquistador who destroyed the empire of the Incas.
What makes the thought of dying so unbearable is that

we have never fully lived. What makes us struggle so desperately against the threat of becoming nothing is our failure to become anything sure and clear, our shadowy identity. So we cling to the things that seem to give us more substance, we grasp competitively at the possessions or the reputation or the status or the power that augment our feeble realities and give us an illusion of being alive.

What seems to have made Jesus of Nazareth so distinctive in the eyes of his fellow Galileans was his intense aliveness. This characteristic is not, perhaps, directly mentioned because it is a rather modern concept. But I believe it is a justifiable observation. To be alive is to be aware of what others, less alive, have failed to notice. To be alive is to see ordinary things in an extraordinary way, to be sensitive to new truth, to respond flexibly to unforeseen demands. Jesus has an almost uncanny awareness, it would seem, of the significance of things, of the glory and ugliness of life, of people and their unspoken needs and, above all, the reality of God. Was it not this quality that underlay the verdict of the common people, that he spoke with an intrinsic authority and not as the scribes who had to support everything they affirmed with quotations from scripture or tradition? Wasn't it this inner aliveness that he passed on with a word or a touch to those whose bodily or mental vitality was running down? "Lord, to whom shall we go? Your words are words that give unending life."

The Fourth Gospel, from which of course that quotation comes, makes this its central, recurring theme, and if, as I still believe, it contains an element of eyewitness tradition, I see no reason to regard this theme of life-giving as purely theological reflection.

Theological truth may have been suggested by biographical actuality; Jesus' human personality was such that someone who had fallen under his spell could readily say: "In him was life", or put into his mouth the words "Because I am alive you shall be alive also."

What we are witnessing as we stand before the crucified Christ is not a death but life — life so vividly and intensely alive that it meets death and goes down into nothingness and contains both death and annihilation, taking them in its stride. Death is swallowed up.

Think, if you like, of the aliveness of Jesus as faith. We have dwelt so much on the necessity of our putting our faith in Christ that we lose sight of the prior importance of the faith he put in God and in human beings. So when the darkness of that Friday afternoon offered no assurance of any future and all evidence of a loving God had been taken away, Jesus entrusted himself to hands that had apparently been an illusion. He who cried "Why forsaken?" throws himself into that emptiness, throws himself towards that terrifying absence, calling Father! — saying in effect "I will have it that you are there. I will believe in your love. Let there be God." That naked faith of love is pure aliveness of spirit.

He who is truly alive is free to die. As I have said, the people who find death intolerable are those who have never been more than half alive. The Fourth Gospel again presents Jesus as saying: "No one has robbed me of life. I am laying it down of my own free will. I have the authority to lay it down and I have the authority to receive it back again." Neville Ward has commented: "There was nothing about Jesus that he

wanted to keep. He had found his identity. It is fear of
losing our identity that makes us hold on to life or to
what represents life's meaning for us. At the Cross it is
clear that life is represented by the man who died there
and death by the people who put him there."

In John 12:20-28 we are given the secret of true
aliveness. It comes through the habitual laying down of
life. This is not an insight that belongs to the Fourth
Gospel only: it shines at the centre of the Synoptic
tradition. "Whoever wills to hold on to life is lost. But
if anyone will let themselves be lost, for my sake and
the Gospel, that one is safe. What does a person gain
by winning the whole world at the cost of the true
self?"

Death followed by resurrection, life through dying, is
the way things are. It is not a truth limited to the one
event of Christ's death and resurrection, nor does it
affect us only when we approach the end of our lives. It
is a principle of all existence. Hang on to what you
have of life and you are lost. Let go, do the necessary
dying, and a fuller, richer quality of aliveness will be
given to you.

In any lifetime there are innumerable little deaths
—always painful and frightening — changing house,
seeing a child go away from home for the first time,
losing one's job, leaving one's homeland, the break-up
of a marriage, retirement — you can think of many
more. There are also for every woman and man
occasions when a dying for others is required — one's
own cherished plan surrendered so that someone else
may have a more important breakthrough; one's work
used and the credit given to someone who may need it
more; one's lifestyle curtailed by another's demand
upon us; one's security sacrificed so that others may be

helped. It hardly ever happens with any heroics or romance. It is hard and unacknowledged.

You will know that if you remember some quarrel in which you and your opponents were captured in a mutual deadlock, too convinced or too proud and wounded to make the first move. If in the end you took the first step towards a resolution or reconciliation you know that giving way, admitting your share in the fault, felt like a kind of dying; you were giving up almost more than you could bear. And you may have met with a devastating lack of response, since we are not talking about a technique for success. Yet was it not the case that afterwards you yourself knew that you had become a freer, more confident person, having discovered that you could make a surrender without loss of integrity? The washing of one another's feet, with which we shall symbolically conclude today's meditation, is a striking example of the sort of dying I am describing.[1] To kneel and wash another person's feet entails your submission to some element of humiliation, of servitude, of absurdity. But, equally, to accept the washing of your own feet by someone else means letting go a bit of your self-sufficiency, your privacy, your dignity. Either way, the action brings you to a tiny laying down of life.

If in any of these experiences we acquiesce grudgingly, and with grumbling, we have not laid life down of our own will and should not expect to receive it back again. But a glad letting-go will open the way into a greater fullness of life, though probably of a

---

[1] Footwashing: The ancient practice of footwashing is familiar to some Christians, unfamiliar to others. At the Ecumenical Centre, for some years now we have included footwashing in our worship on Thursday before Easter. As we do so, we recall Jesus' example and teaching, especially on the night before he died (John 13).

quieter and unexpected kind. It is to this pattern of
life through death, the "Jesus principle", that we are
committed by our baptism. As we are reminded in the
familiar words of Romans 6:3-5.

And how may we visualize the little resurrection that
will surely follow each little death? We cannot — that
is the point. It is a real dying, a real annihilation
without guarantee. Look at all those predictions of
his own death which Jesus pronounced. He could see
the inevitable progress of events in detail — handed
over to wicked men, the highpriestly family, handed
on to the Gentiles, the Roman power, flogged, mocked,
spat upon, crucified. But of the new life he could see
nothing but the bare flat statement of faith — "after
three days will rise again". To us also the outcome of
our letting go will remain hidden until it breaks upon
us. We can guess at it only in the impressionistic
terms of such a poem as this:

One day people will touch and talk perhaps easily,
And loving be natural as breathing and warm as
     sunlight,
And people will untie themselves,
     as string is unknotted,
Unfold and yawn and stretch and spread
     their fingers,
Unfurl, uncurl like seaweed returned to the sea,
And work will be simple and swift
     as a seagull flying,
And play will be casual and quiet
     as a seagull settling,
And the clocks will stop, and no-one will wonder
     or care or notice,

And people will smile without reason,
  even in winter, even in the rain.[2]

A Litany

The sufferings of this present time are not worth
comparing with the glory that is to be revealed.
  I saw a new heaven and a new earth, for the
  former things had passed away.

The creation waits with eager longing for the
revealing of the children of God.
  I saw a new heaven and a new earth, for the
  former things had passed away.

The creation was subjected to futility, not of its own
will but by the will of him who subjected it in hope.
  I saw a new heaven and a new earth, for the
  former things had passed away.

The creation itself will be set free from its bondage
to decay and obtain the glorious liberty of the children
of God.
  I saw a new heaven and a new earth, for the
  former things had passed away.

---

[2] "Day Dream", A.S.J. Tessimond, in *Voices in a Giant City* and
Not Love Perhaps, reprinted with permission of Hubert Nicholson
and Autolycus Publications, London.

The whole creation has been groaning in travail together until now: and not only the creation, but we ourselves, who have the first fruit of the Spirit, groan inwardly as we wait for adoption as sons and daughters, the redemption of our bodies.

I saw a new heaven and a new earth, for the former things had passed away. [3]

---

[3] From *Jesus Christ — the Life of the World*, a worship book for the Sixth Assembly of the World Council of Churches, Vancouver 1983, Geneva, WCC, 1983, p. 22.